DEPARTMENT OF THE ENVIRONMENT

CASTLES

An introduction to the
castles of England
and Wales

by the late **B. H. St. J. O'NEIL, M.A., F.S.A.**

*formerly Chief Inspector
of Ancient Monuments*

London

Her Majesty's Stationery Office

1973

ISBN 0 11 670430 6

Contents

Illustrations

Plans

Castles printed in italics in the text
are in the care of the Department
of the Environment.

Castles

The meaning of the word "Castle"

The word "castle" may be seen on English maps against all manner of different sites and buildings, some fortified, some purely residential, from long abandoned prehistoric camps to pseudo-Gothic shams. The usage of the country, on which the makers of the maps relied, is no sure guide in this respect. Yet the confusion in popular memory is hardly surprising, when it is realized that even the early chroniclers, who were the contemporaries of the first true castles, were quite indiscriminate in their use of sundry different terms of description.

Nevertheless it is now clear that the term should not properly be applied to any structure in the British Isles, whether of earth or stone, erected before the conquest of England by the Normans, which was begun at the Battle of Hastings in AD 1066. To this rule, the truth of which was established over a generation ago, there are a very few exceptions, namely those castles which were built by favourites of the English king, Edward the Confessor, about AD 1050; but these men were Normans, the precursors of the later invaders, and their works hardly belie the statement that, whilst England was a Saxon kingdom, castles were unknown this side of the English Channel.

A castle was a private fortress, of king or noble, and was a product of the feudal system. That system, which grew strong and all-embracing from the weakness of the later Carolingian Empire in Western Europe, was based upon the personal service of vassals to the king in return for grants of land or jurisdiction. Many vassals had lesser men owing them allegiance, and each in turn came to seek the protection of a fortress, to which he could retire in case of conflict with his neighbours. For such a system led inevitably to lawlessness except when a strong central government was able to keep the peace between the rival nobles.

This system did not exist in England before the Norman Conquest, although there was already a tendency amongst the Saxons in a direction which might have led to its gradual adoption. After the conquest it was imposed by the conquerors, just as later it was imposed at least in part upon the Welsh and Irish. With this system came its symbol, the private fortress, namely the castle.

The earliest castles

After the Norman Conquest, when William, Duke of Normandy, established himself as King William I of England, castles were built in great numbers. About one hundred are known to have come into existence before AD 1100, and it is probable that there were many more. But their very numbers, and the ease with which they were erected, burnt and re-erected shows that their principal material was wood, not stone.

Most of them were of the type known now as "motte and bailey". The motte was a high mound of earth, shaped like a truncated cone, with a circular, flat top. A ditch surrounded the mound, which was made of the material dug from it. Beyond lay one or more baileys or courtyards, each also surrounded by a ditch which joined that round the motte. The soil thrown up from this ditch was used to make a rampart round the edge of the bailey. The summit of the mound had a stout fence or palisade along its edge and within this there was a wooden tower or house. In the bailey there were other wooden buildings, and access from the bailey to the top of the motte was only possible by means of a sloping bridge across the ditch and up the side of the mound.

The exact time and place of origin of this type of fortification is unknown. The earliest reference to a castle which was perhaps of this type occurs in AD 1010 at a place on the River Loire in France. Its maker, Fulk Nerra, was noted for his skill in military affairs. He is also the first medieval lord who is known to have employed mercenary soldiers, and it cannot be denied that a motte is a fortress for a man who wishes to be able to defend himself, his family and his close associates against all enemies, whether they are neighbouring lords or his own rebellious retainers. Whatever its origin, the style of castle which included a motte came into frequent use in France in the early part of the eleventh century, especially in Normandy during the minority of Duke William, who later conquered England. It was, therefore, only natural that he and his followers should introduce the style into England.

The Bayeux Tapestry, which was made, perhaps in England, late in the eleventh century AD and is preserved at Bayeux in Normandy, shows several of these castles with their towers on the mound and bridge in position, and one being constructed at Hastings in Sussex. The remains of this mound are still visible, but all other parts of Hastings Castle are of later date. The picture of the castle at Dinan shows also how vulnerable such castles were to attacks by fire. Two of the attackers are shown with long torches, attempting to set fire to the palisade round the tower, whilst the defenders above are preparing to repel other attackers on horseback, who are about to cross the bridge. No doubt the defenders did their best to prevent the fire catching by covering the woodwork with wet hides and the like, but their supply of water can seldom have been unlimited, and the many references to the burning of castles show that they often failed. There must have been many tragedies like the burning of the wooden tower on the motte of York Castle, where *Clifford's Tower* now stands. The Jews of York, attacked by a mob, had taken refuge there in 1190, but the tower was burnt and with it many of the refugees.

There are many hundreds of mottes in the British Isles, most of them now just grassy mounds with attendant ditch and bailey, although some of the largest are to be seen incorporated in later castle buildings, *e.g.* at *Carisbrooke* in the Isle of Wight (Fig. 27 and page 12). As the Normans, with their English followers, pushed on into Wales after the conquest of England, mottes there are especially frequent. In Montgomeryshire alone there are at least fifty.

Mottes were erected in the Isle of Man, probably as early as 1098, as a result not of Anglo-Saxon conquest, for Man was then part of the kingdom of Norway, but of influence from England. As feudalism was introduced into Scotland early in the twelfth century, so too was the castle, and mottes occur as far north as Sutherlandshire. They occur also in Ireland as a result of the Anglo-Norman invasion of Ireland by Strongbow in 1169, and even later examples are known. Clearly they were still of use over a century after their introduction to these islands, although building in stone had by then become quite a common practice. They were vulnerable when a determined and puissant enemy came against them but they were cheap and easy to build and must have often served but a temporary use.

It is indeed probable that many of these hundreds of mottes were never intended to be permanent residences of their lord. Some were for officials who administered estates far from the main centre of the lord's authority. Others were probably intended to control certain routes, such as Roman roads then still in use, or important fords, whilst others again may have been erected as bases during a siege of another castle. In many cases it is possible from written records to state or to guess with an approximation to truth who erected or at least who occupied a certain castle in the early Middle Ages, but in many other cases their builders must remain for ever anonymous. Even excavation will not help, although a very careful examination of the summit of a motte sometimes reveals the postholes of the palisade and tower, as was the case at Abinger in Surrey for example.

Not a few of the most important castles in England were originally of motte and bailey type, but were so altered in later centuries, when buildings in stone became common, that the first plan has been obscured. Windsor Castle, and Arundel Castle in Sussex, however, still show the plan to perfection, although the earthworks have been surmounted or even in part replaced by stone walls. In both these cases a circular stone "shell" keep of later date now exists on the motte. The motte may still be seen at *Carisbrooke*

Clifford's Tower, York, 1245

Carisbrooke Castle, Isle of Wight

Castle, Isle of Wight (Fig. 27 and page 12) and at Cardiff Castle, as well as at *Totnes Castle* in Devon, and at *Clifford's Tower, York* (Fig. 23 and page 12), already mentioned above. At Warkworth in Northumberland, where the castle is one of the most instructive examples of the gradual strengthening of fortifications against improved methods of attack, the motte is still partly preserved beneath a much later great tower (Fig. 28).

It was at *Berkhamsted* that the English finally submitted to Duke William of Normandy, and the castle there may well have been one of the first constructed by the invaders (Fig. 1). It is of motte and bailey type, and, although much masonry was added later, this is now so ruined that the original works are as clearly visible as anywhere in the country. The motte is about 45 ft high with a diameter of 60 ft at the top, and the oblong bailey measures 450 ft by 300 ft. Both are surrounded by wet moats. It is clear that the moats of this type of castle, as of others of later date, were designed to hold water, if it could be obtained by natural means, but there were many cases where no water existed or where owing to the nature of the rock or subsoil it would not remain for any length of time. The motte at *Thetford Castle*, Norfolk, 80 ft high, is probably the highest still remaining, but there are others in the eastern parts of England little less in height, such as those of Ongar (Fig. 2) and Pleshey (Fig. 3), both in Essex.

Although motte and bailey castles of this type were by far the most common erected by the Normans and their imitators in England and Wales, earthworks of a slightly different kind were also employed in certain places. Sometimes the circular area selected for the chief timber buildings was not raised above the adjacent countryside, but was girt by a rampart of earth dug from the surrounding ditch. This was probably the form of the first castle of *Old Sarum* near Salisbury, and of *Restormel Castle* near Lostwithiel, Cornwall (Fig. 7) and fortifications of this kind have been found under later stone walls at *Llawhaden Castle*, Pembrokeshire and *Ogmore Castle*, Glamorgan. In the latter case the area seems to have been oval rather than circular, as may still be seen at Caesar's Camp, Folkestone, which is misleadingly named, whilst at *Kidwelly Castle*, Carmarthenshire (page 24) the area defended was semi-circular, the diameter of the semi-circle being formed by the natural defence provided by a steep cliff to a river.

Much has been written here about mottes and other types of earthen castles of the Normans, because it is necessary to emphasize their importance in the study of fortification in the British Isles. They are ubiquitous in these islands today, because they were the normal type of fortress for a century after the Norman Conquest. Introduced at first as a means of repressing the English and making the conquest permanent, they quickly became a menace to all save the strongest kings. During the Anarchy in the reign of Stephen (1135–54), when the Chronicles record that men said openly "that Christ slept and His Saints", the land was filled with castles, and there is little doubt that many of them were mottes. Most of these "adulterine", *i.e.* unlicensed, castles were destroyed when Henry II came to the throne in 1154.

Early stone castles

Nevertheless mottes were not the only castles built, even in the eleventh century. Just as in Normandy, where stone castles existed early in that century, so in England a few were erected in stone very soon after 1066. The foremost of these was the *Tower of London*, then, as now, the chief castle of the realm. The White Tower, as the keep or Great Tower is called from its white-washed appearance in the Middle Ages, was begun during the reign of William I, but took several years to build. Although much altered in later centuries, it still shows the normal arrangements in such great towers, except that the original entrance at first-floor level through a doorway in the south wall is now a window. The stair to it was external and has disappeared. The ground floor of the tower was used only for storage. The first floor had the principal rooms, the floor above being used as the private apartments for the king and his family. It is obvious that much in the way of comfort was sacrificed for security, but on peaceful occasions there would be no need to resort to the great tower. Other buildings in the bailey below would be in use. The keep of Colchester Castle, Essex, is similar in most respects to the White Tower and is of the same date, but is even larger in plan. Unfortunately it has lost its two upper stages. These two great towers are the only examples of their kind which are known to have been built in the eleventh century. So far as can be ascertained all other keeps belong to the twelfth century.

There are, however, a few castles of which the curtain wall of stone can be shown to belong to a date soon after the Norman Conquest. As a rule they are on rocky sites, where stone was quickly and easily obtainable, so that it was as economical to use as timber. *Richmond Castle* in Yorkshire (Fig. 4) has such a curtain on two sides of the triangular great court, the other side having a steep cliff as a natural defence. In the curtain at the apex of the triangle there is a contemporary gateway, which forms the lowest part of the later keep. Ludlow Castle in Shropshire (Fig. 5) also has an eleventh-century stone curtain, but in this case not only is there a gateway within a tower, later converted into a keep, but there are in addition rectangular towers which project a slight

distance from the curtain. From these the defenders could command with their fire some parts of the curtain. *Peveril Castle*,
Derbyshire (Fig. 6) and *Brough Castle*, Westmorland, are other
examples which have eleventh-century stone curtains, still in part
remaining. *Restormel Castle*, Cornwall (Fig. 7), which has been
quoted already as a good example of an early earthen castle, had
from the beginning a gateway of stone, the remains of which may
still be seen. The most vulnerable part of any fortification is its
entrance, and it is only natural that defenders habitually expend
much of their energy upon making it secure, either by elaboration
of defensive devices or, as in this case, by building it of stone,
whilst all the remainder of the defence was of earth and timber.
It is probable that the first parts of the defences of the town of
Southampton (Fig. 19) to be built of stone were the isolated gate-
ways at the north and east, of which the former remains, em-
bedded in later work. Although few such examples of mixed stone
and earthen defences are now to be found above ground, there
must have been many in the Middle Ages; even in the sixteenth
century Oslo in Norway had wooden defences except for the gate-
ways, which were of stone.

Medieval sieges

During the twelfth century more and more castles were built of
stone, many with rectangular keeps, the characteristic style of the
century, but some without a keep in the manner just described.
The increase was due primarily, not to the increase of wealth and
power of the barons, but to the greater efficiency of the weapons
of attack which forced the defenders to protect themselves with
more solid construction. The acquisition of Jerusalem by the
Turks and the militant Christianity of the Northmen, leading to
the First Crusade in 1096, opened the eyes of the western nations
to the devices commonly used in sieges in the East. Hitherto,
although they were not ignorant of the methods in use in the later
years of the Roman Empire in the West, they seem seldom to have
employed them. Fire and an impetuous onslaught or blockade were
the normal methods employed. Against a wooden castle such tactics
were often successful, but in the Levant against stone castles they
were insufficient. Consequently the Crusaders learnt to construct
large siege engines as a natural corollary of war, not only when on
Crusade, but also in their homelands when they returned. As a
defence against such weapons they regularly built themselves castles
of stone.

The conduct of a siege under these conditions first of all invol-
ved the filling of the ditch in front of the castle with any material

available. This was done under covering fire from the bows and
stone-throwing engines of the attackers. Then various methods were
used to effect a breach in the stone curtain. A direct assault might be
made with a battering ram or a heavy bore might be applied to the
foundations, or sappers might be set to work to undermine a section
of the wall. In any or all of these devices the machinery and the men
were protected by means of stout penthouses from the heavy missiles
and combustibles hurled down from the wall-top by the defenders.
The latter also endeavoured to divert the blow of the ram by catching
its head in a forked beam or a hook. The defenders had also sometimes to contend with a "belfry", a high wooden movable tower,
which after the moat had been filled could be wheeled up to the
castle. From this the attackers could rake the top of the curtain
with their arrows and could sometimes let down a sort of drawbridge and so storm the castle. Another method of storming a
castle was by simple escalade, a daring, but not impossible, pro-
cedure used when covering fire from without forced the defenders
off the wall-top, from which alone could they thrust away the
ladders placed against the curtain.

To combat these devices the builders of castles adopted various
expedients. An obvious improvement was to build higher walls,
high enough in fact to prohibit escalade or the use of a "belfry"
because of the great height which would be required. Another
necessity was to gain command over the berm or space immediately in front of the curtain, since this was the site of most of the
attackers' devices. In some castles, especially in France but not
often certainly noted in England, covered wooden galleries or
hoardings were built out from the wall-top, supported on hori-
zontal wooden brackets. The holes for these timbers may sometimes be seen on the outside of castle walls. From these galleries,
which had holes in their floors, missiles could be dropped directly
on to any attackers who were at the base of the wall.

A more effective way of gaining command of the berm was to
build towers or turrets projecting from the curtain, because from
them it was possible for archers, firing along the wall, to enfilade
any attackers who had gained a foothold there. Towers of this
kind have already been noted on the eleventh-century curtain at Ludlow Castle (Fig. 5), but they were insufficient in number for complete command. A much better example—of later date—is the
curtain of *Framlingham Castle*, Suffolk (1190–1200) (Fig. 8 and
page 17), which has thirteen rectangular towers projecting from a
high curtain. It may here be remarked that the siege engines, which
medieval armies inherited from the Roman Empire, namely the
ballista, which was a gigantic bow for shooting huge bolts, and the
mangonel, which hurled large stones and other missiles, had been

Framlingham Castle, Suffolk, 1190–1200

reinforced by the thirteenth century by the trebuchet, which was
an enormous mechanical sling. This had a high trajectory, which
enabled it to throw missiles into a castle. The reply of the besieged
to this new weapon was to build even higher walls.

Rectangular keeps

Rectangular keeps, or Great Towers, as they were called by their
contemporaries, are amongst the most imposing remains of the
Middle Ages in Britain. Like their predecessors, the mottes, they
were chiefly intended as a last refuge in time of war in case the
enemy stormed or breached the curtain. They are indeed transla-
tions into stone of the wooden towers, which stood on mottes,
but because of their weight they were very seldom placed actually on
the earlier mounds. Instead, as a defensive device, they have their
only entrance door at first-floor level.

Two of the most imposing keeps, those of London and Colchester,
have already been mentioned, because they were built in the
eleventh century. The keep of *Rochester Castle* seems to have
been begun about 1127, and that of *Ogmore Castle*, Glamorgan,
has detailed decoration which shows that it was built early in the
twelfth century. Excavations have shown that small rectangular
keeps were built at Lydney in Gloucestershire and Ascot D'Oyly
in Oxfordshire during the reign of Stephen (1135–54), and there
is a suggestion that another such keep was erected at this time at
Membury in Wiltshire. It may be, therefore, that not a few of the
"adulterine" castles of that troubled reign included such small
rectangular keeps. Nevertheless it remains the truth that, in general,
rectangular keeps were a product of the reign of Henry II (1154–89).
This king set himself to compel the destruction of the many unlicensed castles of the previous reign, and in their stead himself raised
a number of imposing great towers, which he kept in his own hands
as royal castles. Some others were built by wealthy nobles with the
king's permission.

A list of some of the most important remaining rectangular keeps,
as of other types of castles, will be found at the end of this book. No
two rectangular keeps are exactly alike, but all are closely similar in
many respects, both externally and internally. As a rule they are—or
at least originally were—greater in height than in length or breath,
e.g. Portchester, Hampshire (Fig. 9 and page 18). Most of them have
shallow buttresses at the angles and in the centre of each side, which
at the bottom die away into a splayed or battered base. The roof had
a steep pitch, and was entirely hidden from below by high parapets;
very often the steep roof was replaced by a flatter one at a later time,
in order to add another storey to the accommodation in the keep.

As already mentioned, the entrance was generally at first-floor level; in some cases it was even higher. Many keeps had ground level entrances inserted at a later date, *e.g. Goodrich* (Fig. 16 and page 23). The approach to the entrance was by means of a stair, which rose beside one of the walls of the keep, often within a forebuilding, which sometimes had its own defences. A chapel, which was normally included in a keep, was sometimes in this forebuilding. The entrance opened directly into the interior, usually into the principal room of the building. In the larger keeps, *e.g. Middleham*, Yorkshire (Fig. 10), a cross-wall divided this room and the other rooms above and below into two unequal portions, but this was primarily devised in order that there should not be too great a span for the floors. These were invariably of wood, vaults over the main rooms being unknown in this class of building. Smaller rooms were sometimes contrived in the walls of keeps, where those were particularly thick, quite apart from the narrow passages leading to garderobes (latrines), which are sometimes—but quite wrongly—shown to visitors as prison cells! A well is normally found in a keep and fireplaces are usual, but a room which can be described as a kitchen is seldom, if ever, found. When no fireplace remains, it must be supposed that heat was obtained from movable braziers.

Access from floor to floor within the keep was normally by means of a spiral stair in an angle of the building. The ground floor was accessible only by this means from the floor above and was used for storage. Stories about its use as a prison should never be believed without the strongest corroborative evidence, which is seldom forthcoming. Confusion has arisen from the contemporary name for these great towers. "Keep" is a modern term. In ancient times these towers were referred to as "donjon", a word now corrupted into "dungeon," which has a modern meaning quite different from that of the word from which it is derived.

Some of the smaller keeps, like that of *Peveril Castle*, Derbyshire (Fig. 6), and *Coity Castle*, Glamorgan (Fig. 12), had very little accommodation within them. They are of the same general type as the large keeps, but they cannot have been intended as permanent residences, even for a constable who was in charge for the royal owner. In the case of *Peveril* the remains have been found of a hall and other buildings close to the keep, and there is no doubt that these were the normal accommodation in use, the keep being saved for emergencies. In other cases, however, the keep is so large and so well appointed, that it may have been in general use. This is but one example of the difficulty, which will be referred to from time to time, of deciding how much the plan of a particular castle may have been dictated by the needs of defence and how much by the desire for comfort. For it must always be remembered that in most cases castles were residences as well as fortifications; sometimes indeed it is difficult to decide whether a building should be classed as a castle or merely as a house with defences.

Shell keeps

It has been mentioned that rectangular keeps were very seldom built on the top of mottes. In some castles, however, which never had a rectangular keep, the palisade round the summit of the motte was replaced by a stone wall or curtain, round or polygonal in plan. Within the small courtyard thus enclosed, which is sometimes called a shell keep, there were buildings of stone or wood, abutting against the wall. As a rule the palisade round the bailey was replaced at the same time by a stone curtain, which was carried up the slope of the motte in two places, to join the wall of the shell keep. Excellent examples of this kind of keep are to be found in the castles of Arundel, Windsor, Cardiff, *Carisbrooke* (Isle of Wight) (Fig. 27 and page 12), *Pickering* (Yorkshire) and the West Country castles of *Totnes* in Devon and *Launceston*, *Restormel* (Fig. 7) and Trematon in Cornwall.

In a few cases the stone curtain of the shell keep was not built on the top of the motte but on the ground at its base, and was carried up as a revetment wall to the whole mound. The most celebrated example is at Berkeley Castle, in Gloucestershire, which has a forebuilding covering the entrance like a rectangular keep but there are others at *Farnham Castle*, Surrey, and Carmarthen Castle.

Mines and the remedy

Few of the methods of siege warfare, already described, could be used against such massive structures as the rectangular keeps. But there was one to which they were vulnerable, namely mining. A sap or gallery could be driven beneath and across a corner of the rectangle, provided always that the sappers were adequately protected against the defenders' fire. They would insert wooden props as they went along. When the gallery had been completed, fire would be lit therein, to destroy the props, with the result that the corner above would collapse and expose the inside of the keep. Just such a gallery has been found beneath an angle of the keep of Bungay Castle, Suffolk. It seems not to have been dug during an actual siege, but to have been ordered by Henry II as a means of destroying the keep after its surrender.

As a counter to this method of attack the builders of castles took various precautions. At *Kenilworth Castle*, Warwickshire (Fig. 11), for instance, the buttresses which clasp the corners of the keep project so far from the main faces of the walls, that they almost form small towers. They are solid up to the first floor. It is doubtful whether any mine of the kind described would have affected their stability. Another device employed was to build small tower-like projections on to the middle of each side of the keep. These occur at Castle Rushden, Isle of Man, and are solid up to the first floor. They would make it exceedingly difficult for sappers ever to reach a position from which to drive a gallery under one of the main corners of the keep, whilst the projections themselves were invulnerable to mining. The keep of *Orford Castle*, Suffolk, built between 1165 and 1167, is slightly earlier than some of the rectangular keeps, but it shows an advance in planning which they never exhibit. It is said to have been an object of especial delight to Henry II. It is circular internally, but polygonal externally and has three large rectangular turrets projecting from it, from which flanking fire could be directed to command the whole face of the main tower. At *Conisbrough Castle*, Yorkshire, the keep (1185–90), which is one of the finest monuments of the Middle Ages in England, is circular in plan, but from it there project six solid buttresses, which rise in front of the sloping base of the main tower. From the summit of these turrets it was possible to command the whole of the area immediately in front of the keep, whilst the sloping base itself kept attackers from approaching very close. It had also the advantage that stones dropped from above would rebound from its surface at unpredictable angles, to the discomfiture of attackers who had approached near to the tower.

Round towers

The circular form of the two last-mentioned keeps introduces a new feature in the development of fortifications, devised in reply to improved methods of attack, that is, the use of curved surfaces of wall-face on the outside of towers. It has already been noted that the vulnerable points of rectangular keeps were their angles. This was because, however well bounded the masonry may be, there is always a tendency for it to fall outwards at such points. A wall which lacks such angles is stronger. All the masonry is of equal strength and solidity, and mines are less likely to be successful against it than against structures with angles.

The curved wall-face in towers, whether circular, semi-circular or D-shaped, was almost universal in castles of the thirteenth century and persisted in later centuries until the influence of cannon caused great modifications in the form of fortification. But its introduction

Kidwelly Castle, Carmarthenshire

into England occurred at a time when the keep, as a last resort in defence, was still considered of value. There are, therefore, to be found a certain number of circular keeps dating from *c*. AD 1200. The best example is at Pembroke, which was a base for English expeditions to Ireland. It is 75 ft high, almost intact except for its wooden floors, and, like other of its class, resembles the rectangular keeps in having its entrance at first-floor level. In Monmouthshire and the adjacent parts of Herefordshire and Breconshire there are several other such round keeps, all smaller than that of Pembroke and all built upon mottes. The most impressive are those of Caldicot and *Skenfrith* (Monmouthshire) (Fig. 13), *Bronllys* and *Tretower* (Breconshire) and Longtown (Herefordshire), all dating from early in the thirteenth century. The Welsh Princes in North Wales, constantly fighting for their independence against the English, were not backward in adopting the latest military devices of their opponents. Just as at *Dolwyddelan* in Caernarvonshire one of them built a rectangular keep, which is contemporary with such buildings in England (*c*. 1170), so at *Dolbadarn* in the same county (Fig. 14) they built a round keep early in the following century.

There are a few examples of keeps which have one curved side, the remainder being straight. They are clearly experiments, made at a time when men were searching for improvements in fortification without full knowledge of the devices which elsewhere had already been shown to be of value. The keep of *Helmsley Castle* (Yorkshire) (*c*. 1200) is of this type, and once more the work of the native princes of Wales provides an example at *Ewloe Castle*, Flintshire, which may be dated *c*. 1210.

Keeps of circular form are few in number compared with their rectangular predecessors, because by the time they came to be devised engineers were concentrating upon strengthening the defences of the curtain and dispensing altogether with a keep. Keeps were immensely strong, but their defence was largely passive with the limited range of the bows then in use. A strong curtain not only gave greater protection to the living quarters which were by now regularly built in the courtyard instead of sometimes being confined to the keep, but also gave a much wider field of fire to the defenders for purposes of counter-attack. But to be strong the curtain must be high to make escalade difficult, and must be provided with towers at regular intervals, from which by flanking fire the defenders could enfilade the whole of its base and the berm in front. For reasons already mentioned a curved wall-face is stronger than an angular one when there is danger of mining being employed by the attackers. It followed from this that the normal, although not the only, form of towers on the curtain from now onwards for two centuries was curved to the field, that is, to the direction of attack.

The castles of the thirteenth century

The earliest towers with a rounded front were made solid, such as those on the curtain of *Conisbrough*, built soon after the erection of the keep, *c.* 1200, and those of the gatehouse of Longtown Castle (Herefordshire), but very soon they were built hollow, in order to provide additional accommodation, or to give extra fighting platforms flanking the curtain, or for both reasons. *White Castle, Skenfrith* (Fig. 13) and *Grosmont Castles*, the three castles in Monmouthshire, which belonged to the Justiciar, Hubert de Burgh, have good examples of semi-circular mural towers of the period 1220–40. In the first case they were added to the front of the twelfth-century curtain, doorways to the towers being broken through it; in the other two castles there was no earlier stone curtain and the towers were built with a new wall and gatehouse. A somewhat earlier example of the same kind of defence occurs at *Helmsley Castle*, Yorkshire, whilst the very fine medieval curtain and towers of the inner ward of *Pevensey Castle*, Sussex, date from about 1250 (Fig. 15 and page 27). The towers of Pevensey are D-shaped internally instead of circular; this was a development often found in the latter part of the thirteenth century, which gave more space in the rooms of the tower without detracting from their solidity. The inner curtain of the *Tower of London* and the outer curtain of *Dover Castle* are particularly good examples of the thirteenth-century style of forti-fication, which enabled the defenders to command all parts of the enceinte of a castle. As a rule the ground floor of the towers was reached from the courtyard as at *Goodrich*, Herefordshire (Fig. 16 and page 23), but there was no communication thence upwards to higher floors. These were entered from the wall-walk on the top of the curtain, which as a rule passed through them. The tendency was more and more to make each tower into a potential stronghold by itself. An enemy by escalade or breach might eventually gain access to part of the wall-walk or the courtyard, but he still had not gained the castle, even one which lacked a keep as a last resort. For the de-fenders could still hold out in the mural towers, which with stout doors across the wall-walk prohibited him from gaining the whole curtain in one assault. Each tower had to be captured in turn.

During this period of development of medieval fortification much attention was devoted to the defences of the entrance. As a rule there was only one large gateway to a castle, although some had two and many had a small postern for eventual escape of the defenders, if they were beaten; this was usually in a position difficult of access from outside. The normal gatehouse of the thirteenth century, as at *Pevensey* (Fig. 15), consists of an entrance flanked on each side by large, high towers, semi-circular in front but straight-sided towards the courtyard within. The ditch in front of the entrance was crossed

Pevensey Castle, Sussex,
inner ward, c. 1250

Dover Castle, Kent

by a wooden bridge, which was movable. This is usually called a drawbridge, but the term should not properly be used for the type normally used in this century. Unlike later bridges, they were not drawn upwards by means of chains, but were pivoted, like a see-saw, on an axle, the recesses for the ends of which may often be seen in the sides of the towers flanking the entrance. A better name for this device is turning-bridge. Heavy weights attached to the inner end of such a bridge caused it to swing to a vertical position, prohibiting entrance, except when it was fixed horizontally by means of bolts.

Immediately within the bridge was the portcullis, an iron-shod wooden grille which could be let down through a groove from an upper floor of the gatehouse. Beyond this was the door, which led into the actual entrance passage. This was often covered by a stone vault, in which there were holes through which defenders above could assail any besiegers who had won their way so far. Similar holes often occur in the parapet at the top of the outer face of the gatehouse, and many are the stories told of molten lead being poured from above. All of these stories are modern elaborations, calculated to improve upon the truth. Lead was just as precious in the Middle Ages as now, and its employment for such a purpose strikes one as unnecessarily expensive, especially when a heavy stone could be just as unpleasant a missile. The entrance passage was as a rule commanded by means of arrow-slits from the guard-chambers, which were in the ground floor of the flanking towers. In later examples there was often another door, opening inwards, and another portcullis towards the inner end of the passage, but these were normally provided only when the gatehouse itself was regarded as the strongest part of the castle; this is a development which will be referred to below. The upper floors of the gatehouse were used for defensive purposes, such as for working the portcullis and for the quarters of the garrison, but in later examples provided accommodation for the constable or whoever controlled the castle. There are many fine examples of thirteenth-century gatehouses, such as those of *Pevensey Castle*, Sussex (Fig. 15), *Criccieth Castle*, Caernarvonshire, and *White Castle*, Monmouthshire; other examples will be found in the list at the end of this book.

The Edwardian castles of North Wales

In the past few pages many examples have been quoted from castles in Wales and the Marches. This is because almost constant warfare between Welsh and English in the thirteenth century led to much building of strongholds and development of fortifications. And it is to Wales that one must turn for the most perfect specimens in these islands of medieval fortifications, the castles built by Edward I after the Welsh campaigns of 1277 and 1282.

The castles built by this king, of which there are substantial remains, are at *Flint*, *Rhuddlan* (Flintshire), *Conwy*, *Caernarvon* (page 31), *Beaumaris* (Anglesey) (page 31), *Harlech* (Merioneth), and Aberystwyth (Cardiganshire). In each case, except *Harlech*, a fortified town was included in the original design. The walls of *Conwy* and *Caernarvon* (Fig. 20) are still practically intact, and the whole system, castle, town wall and town plan of the former is one of the finest of its kind in Europe.

The perfection and magnificence of these examples of the work of the medieval engineer must be seen to be believed. They have high curtains, adequately flanked by towers, usually round, and most elaborately defended entrances. At *Caernarvon* (Fig. 17) and *Conwy* there is a single defended area, divided into two by a cross-wall, and *Flint Castle* has a peculiar plan, for which there is no parallel of its date (1277). But the other examples quoted are all built on a concentric plan, *e.g.* *Beaumaris* (Fig. 18). The inner ward, of immense height except now at Aberystwyth Castle, which is much ruined, has towers on the curtain and one or more gatehouses. Parallel with this wall and as a rule only a few yards outside it is another, the outer curtain, which also had towers flanking its line. This is always much lower than the inner curtain; at *Harlech* and *Rhuddlan* it is only a few feet high. The purpose of this was to enable the defenders on the inner curtain to fire over the heads of those on the outer curtain without hurting them. Quite often the towers of the outer curtain were left open at the back, in order that, if taken by an enemy, they would be of little use to him, because their interior would be under fire from the inner curtain.

The castles of Edward I in North Wales are the most celebrated of those of concentric type, but they are by no means the only examples. Other castles were assimilated to this style in the thirteenth century by the addition of an outer curtain. The *Tower of London* shows this system splendidly, as do Castle Rushden, Isle of Man, and *Kidwelly Castle*, Carmarthenshire, one of the finest of the many castles of South Wales (page 24). But for elaboration of this system, where water was available for wide moats and lakes, and for intricate defences of the entrance one must go to *Caerphilly Castle* in Glamorgan, which is rightly prized as the greatest castle in the British Isles.

The erection of these masterpieces of fortification was the result of the wisdom and the success of the great English king, Edward I. His reign (1272–1307), together with those of his son, Edward II (1307–27), and grandson, Edward III (1327–77), covers a complete century during much of which the English were supreme at war throughout north-western Europe. Wales was conquered. The Scots were overcome, although not conquered, and much of France was overrun and annexed. The expeditions which accomplished these feats had amongst them most of the warlike spirits of the land, who, whilst away at foreign wars, had little thought for private quarrels at home. Thus it came about that there was less need in the fourteenth century than there had been in the preceding hundred years for the private fortress called castle.

Another feature of contemporary life tended in the same direction. Growth of trade went hand in hand with the expansion of domain, and with it there grew up a class of traders, living in towns, who quickly made themselves as important as the nobles in the councils of the realm. Their power was based on their wealth, which had, of course, to be stored in their towns. These, therefore, needed defences, and it is amongst town walls as much as amongst castles that fourteenth-century fortification is to be seen. Some towns, of course, already had defences, but in many cases they were of earth and timber except for a stone gateway, and in some they were incomplete. The town wall of York is almost complete, but is hardly typical, although it is most imposing with its turreted gates, called Bars. The wall of Great Yarmouth is entirely a work of the fourteenth century or later, and is very well preserved. In even better preservation, because more visible today, is the wall of Southampton (Fig. 19), a product of a hundred years' work from about 1260 onwards. The walls of *Conwy* and *Caernarvon* (Fig. 20) surrounding the boroughs founded by Edward I, when he built the adjacent castles, are practically intact, and so is the less well-known wall of the town of Tenby in Pembrokeshire. The system is the same in almost all cases. There is a high wall, the face of which could everywhere be observed, and, if necessary, defended from towers projecting at suitable intervals along its course. These towers are usually D-shaped and are hollow. Often they had no back wall and were in fact mere fighting platforms. Such a tower on the wall of Canterbury was once again fitted up for use in the original manner, with a movable wooden floor, in the year 1940.

For these and other reasons the domiciles of the nobles of England from now onwards tended to become less and less martial in appearance. It is not easy in certain cases to decide whether a building should be called a castle because of a few signs of fortification, or whether one should rest content with the term defended house. It is not possible to define a line between the two, because at all times there were infinite gradations. Even in Northumberland in the late thirteenth century there existed a very lightly defended house, Aydon Castle; elsewhere in England there were many more. Many of them in these later centuries were enclosed within areas, rectangular and often square, defined by a wet moat. The grassy

Beaumaris Castle, Anglesey,
1295–1330

remains of these, their buildings long since vanished, are to be seen in hundreds in the eastern counties, labelled "Moat" on the Ordnance Survey maps. They are poorer relations of such a structure as Maxstoke Castle in Warwickshire, which is still inhabited. It is square in plan, is surrounded by a moat, and was certainly capable of defence, but its prime purpose was the comfort of its lord.

Stokesay Castle, Shropshire, is an interesting case in point. Its owner, Lawrence of Ludlow, received licence to crenellate it on 19th October, 1290. This term means that he was entitled to put battlements on to the top of the walls, in other words to fortify it, since without proper battlements adequate defence would be difficult. Because of this licence Stokesay is called and is looked upon as castle, but in actual fact its only fortification is a strong tower next to the southern end of the hall. All the other buildings are of an entirely domestic character.

The English house of the Middle Ages

It will be well here to mention the normal plan of an English house of this date. It is remarkably uniform; whether in castle or mere house, large and small, the main features remain constant. The hub of the whole was the hall, either on the ground floor, or raised on a cellar and approached by steps, and open to the roof. Here all met for meals and on other occasions, and here in early days no doubt many slept. The lord and his family ate at a table back to one end of the hall, placed on a dais or slightly raised platform. Other tables were set lengthwise down the hall below the dais. In early days an open hearth blazed in the centre of the floor, the smoke escaping through a hole in the roof. This system persisted for many years, and may be seen at Penshurst Place in Kent, long after wall fireplaces had already become known.

At the lower end of the hall was a screen to keep out draughts; for here were two doors, one in each long wall, and these were the principal method of entry into the hall. The passage between the two doors is called the screens passage. It is often covered by the floor of a gallery above, wherein minstrels sometimes played. Off the screens passage in the end wall of the hall there were doors leading to buttery and pantry and by means of a passage to the kitchen beyond. Above the buttery and pantry there was sometimes a fine room.

The best rooms of the house were, however, reserved for the lord, who could retire from the high table through a door in the upper end wall of the hall to his solar or withdrawing room. In early days this was usually on the first floor. Other rooms and a chapel were often added to this wing of the house.

This was the Englishman's house of the later Middle Ages, and many are the examples, often varied in plan according to the site, which may be found in English castles of nearly all types.

Castles of livery and maintenance

The English prowess in war, which has been mentioned, was accomplished by means not of the feudal levy, the body of men pledged to give a certain number of days' service to their lord in return for certain privileges, but by the use of mercenaries, armed bands paid to do their master's bidding. Any system of this kind has—or can have—an evil consequence, namely a tendency on the part of the hirelings to desert one master for another who will pay them more for their services. Fear of revolt was, therefore, a constant menace during the later Middle Ages in Europe, and had a profound effect upon the plan of later castles. In England the results of this tendency may be seen in castles as early as the reign of Edward I, but they become more obvious after the war in France had gone badly for the English, c. 1370–80. This was because of the presence in this country of a large number of professional soldiers of fortune; this is the particular age of the "castles of livery and maintenance", as they are called.

The principle adopted for building at this time was not unlike that used in the eleventh century in the erection of motte and bailey castles, and perhaps for somewhat the same reason (page 9). The lord made certain of the security of his own quarters and often made sure that the chief defensive point, the entrance, was directly under his control. It was essential that, should his garrison become mutinous, he could still hold his castle, or at least remain safe himself in his own quarters. Various means were adopted to this end, but one feature is always incorporated in them, namely the absence or at least severe restriction of access from the retainers' quarters to the lord's quarters.

An early manifestation of this type of castle-planning is to be seen in the gatehouse of some of the Edwardian castles in North Wales, such as *Harlech*. This building is a self-contained block, defended at ground level by no less than three portcullises and two doorways. There was no access between ground floor and first floor, so that, even if the portcullises and doorways fell, the remainder of the building did not necessarily capitulate. Access from outside to its upper part was by means of an external stair to a doorway at first-floor level. Within the gatehouse was accommodation equivalent to that of a complete house. It was the residence of the Constable, who thereby had under his direct control the chief point of the castle, for both defence and attack, and was also able to keep a strict eye on the remainder of the garrison in the courtyard below. At *Dunstanburgh Castle*, Northumberland (Fig. 21), there is a great gatehouse of this kind.

At a somewhat later date there were built in some castles strong towers, which at first sight closely resemble twelfth-century keeps. They were built that way not because it was the fashion to copy the old, as has been suggested; military men do not build for reasons of that sort. Moreover the accommodation in such towers is seldom convenient. There must have been a compelling necessity which brought them into being, and there is no doubt that it was this same fear of mutinous mercenaries. Towers like that at *Ashby de la Zouch Castle*, Leicestershire, *Raglan Castle*, Monmouthshire, and Tattershall Castle, Lincolnshire, and even *Nunney Castle*, Somerset (1373) (Fig. 22 and page 35), are good examples. So are the towers now newly built on top of earlier mottes at *Warkworth Castle*, Northumberland (Fig. 28), at Dudley Castle, Worcestershire, and at York Castle, where *Clifford's Tower* (Fig. 23 and page 12) is another specimen of the same development. All were establishments for the lord which could, if necessary, be self-sufficient, regardless of the retainers in the courtyards below.

Introduction of firearms

This is not the place to dilate upon the influence of firearms on the practice of war. Cannon existed in 1326. They were almost certainly in use at the battle of Crécy in 1346, but it was many years before they were the really decisive element in battle, and by that time true castles had ceased to be erected. They had been superseded by forts and fortifications. But by 1380 the English who, if they had not in fact invented the new weapon, had at least learnt of its potentialities in the later stages of the recent war in France, were in fear of invasion by the French. Defence of the coast became an urgent necessity, and it is in the defences of these times that gunports for cannon first make their appearance. They resemble that usual medieval arrow-slit externally except that the lower end has a circular expansion, giving the whole opening the shape of a keyhole. Such gunports occur earliest in Canterbury Westgate (1380) and Cooling Castle Inner Gatehouse (1381), both in Kent.

There is one castle which combines within itself many of the features described in the last few pages, with the result that it is of particular importance in the study of castles. This is Bodiam Castle, Sussex. Built in 1386 for coastal defence, it has in its gatehouse gunports of keyhole design, and of two sizes. The accommodation within the curtain is typical of an English house, but the peculiarity is that

St Mawes Castle, Cornwall, c. 1543

Nunney Castle, Somerset

everything is duplicated, and between the two sets of rooms there is no connection. One set was for the lord; the other for his retainers.

Coastal defence

The Civil War of the mid-fifteenth century, known as the Wars of the Roses, had one outstanding result. It destroyed the old nobility. With them went the use of castles as residences; for by the time a new nobility arose under the Tudor dynasty conditions were different. In particular they were more peaceful, and normally a great lord could and did live with perfect security in one of the great houses which now took their place as the successors of the castles.

In one respect only were fortifications required—coastal defence. The policy of this country or of its neighbours led from time to time to a real danger of invasion. There was a particularly bad scare in 1538–40 and again in 1588. On such occasions new defences were as a rule erected to take advantage of better weapons or to guard particularly vulnerable points. Sometimes the work was done by local effort, as at Dartmouth, where *Dartmouth Castle* was built by the Corporation in 1481–94 (Fig. 24). This is the earliest structure to show gunports which have advanced in any real particular from the medieval arrow-slit; they are large rectangular openings. But the castle is not a house in any sense. It is a mere defence post with a little accommodation for a garrison, and, if a castle is rightly defined as a lord's house defended against all comers, this is not a real castle.

The story, therefore, is really at an end, but since there are later military structures which bear the name castle, they should not be altogether omitted. The great scare of 1538–40 led Henry VIII to embark upon an elaborate scheme of coastal defence, and Henry VIII's castles are conspicuous features of the English shore. The whole scheme extended from Hull to Milford Haven, but the chief castles were built in the Thames, where none remain, at *Deal* and *Walmer* (Fig. 25) (two fine examples), at Sandgate, where the castle is in a private garden and was partly removed by the sea many years ago, in the Solent and the Isle of Wight, *Hurst Castle* being the most accessible, and at Falmouth Haven, where *Pendennis Castle* (Fig. 26) and *St Mawes Castle* (page 35) are amongst the best remaining examples of their class. All are low and squat, with thick walls and rounded parapets. There were several tiers of widely splayed embrasures for guns and accommodation for the garrison, but nothing more.

These few pages have been written as an introduction to a very fascinating and very complicated subject. Castles have a great attraction for the English on holiday for a variety of reasons, and many thousands a year pay admission to such a pile as *Caernarvon Castle*. Much in the way of explanation of individual structures is attempted in special guide-books at particular monuments, especially those in the charge of the Department of the Environment. But too often the visitor may miss certain points therein for lack of a general understanding of the purposes of castles in general. It is with this in mind that these pages have been written in an attempt to fill the gap.

Some castles of especial interest

Where a date is given it relates to the building of the particular part of a castle that is under discussion in its category. Other parts are often of different dates. A single date indicates only the beginning of the work.

Castles marked with an asterisk are under the care of the Department of the Environment and most of these are normally open to visitors daily at reasonable hours. Many others also are open to inspection, but appearance in this list is no guarantee of the fact.

MOTTE AND BAILEY CASTLES (Late 11th and early 12th centuries)

*Berkhamsted, Hertfordshire
Brinklow, Warwickshire
Cambridge (1068)
Caerleon, Monmouthshire
Clare, Suffolk
Lewes, Sussex
Lincoln
Ongar, Essex

Oxford
Pleshey, Essex
Shrewsbury, Shropshire
   (1069)
Thetford, Norfolk
Warwick (1068)
*Windsor, Berkshire
*York (two, 1068 and 1069)

See also mottes under Shell Keeps

[N.B. There are many hundreds of these castles, but few are closely dateable]

STONE CURTAINS OF THE 11th CENTURY

*Brough, Westmorland (c. 1095)
Ludlow, Shropshire (1086–95),
   with gatehouse
*Peveril, Derbyshire

*Richmond, Yorkshire
   (c. 1075), with gatehouse
*Rochester, Kent (1087–9)

STONE KEEPS OF THE 11th CENTURY

Colchester, Essex (before 1087)
*Tower of London (begun c. 1077)

STONE KEEPS OF THE EARLY OR MID-12th CENTURY

Ascot D'Oyly, Oxfordshire
   (1130–50)
Corfe, Dorset (c. 1125)
Lydney, Gloucestershire
   (c. 1140)
*Ogmore, Glamorgan (1130–40)

*Pevensey, Sussex (1101–30)
*Rochester, Kent (1126–39)
*Sherborne, Dorset
   (1107–35)

RECTANGULAR STONE KEEPS OF THE LATER 12th CENTURY

Appleby, Westmorland
Bamburgh, Northumberland
   (c. 1160)

*Brough, Westmorland (after
   1174)

*Brougham, Westmorland
  (*c.* 1170–80)
 Bungay, Suffolk (1163–73)
*Carlisle, Cumberland (*c.* 1160)
*Castle Rising, Norfolk
 Chilham, Kent
 Clun, Shropshire
*Coity, Glamorgan
*Deddington, Oxfordshire
*Dolwyddelan, Caernarvonshire
  (*c.* 1170)
*Dover, Kent (1180–86)
*Goodrich, Herefordshire
 Guildford, Surrey
 Hedingham, Essex
*Kenilworth, Warwickshire
  (1160–80)
 Lancaster
 Ludlow, Shropshire
*Lydford, Devon

*Middleham, Yorkshire
  (*c.* 1170)
 Mitford, Northumberland
*Newcastle, Glamorgan
 Newcastle upon Tyne,
  Northumberland (1171–5)
*Norham, Northumberland
  (1160–70)
 Norwich, Norfolk
*Orford, Suffolk (1165–7)
*Peveril, Derbyshire
  (1176–7)
*Portchester, Hampshire
*Prudhoe, Northumberland
*Richmond, Yorkshire
  (*c.* 1171–2)
*Scarborough, Yorkshire
  (1158–64)
 Sutton Valence, Kent
*Wolvesey, Hampshire

SHELL KEEPS OF THE 12th CENTURY

Revetting the motte
 Berkeley, Gloucestershire
 Carmarthen
*Farnham, Surrey
On top of the motte
 Arundel, Sussex
 Brecon
 Cardiff, Glamorgan
*Carisbrooke, Isle of Wight
  (*c.* 1140–50)
 Durham
*Launceston, Cornwall
 Lewes, Sussex
 Lincoln

*Tretower, Breconshire
  (*c.* 1150)

*Pickering, Yorkshire
*Restormel, Cornwall
 Tamworth, Staffordshire
 Tonbridge, Kent
*Totnes, Devon
 Trematon, Cornwall
 Wigmore, Herefordshire
*Windsor, Berkshire
 Wiston, Pembrokeshire

ROUND KEEPS

*Bronllys, Breconshire
 Caldicot, Monmouthshire
*Conisbrough, Yorkshire
  (1185–90)
 Dynevor, Carmarthenshire
*Dolbadarn, Caernarvonshire
  (*c.* 1220)

*Launceston, Cornwall
 Longtown, Herefordshire
 Pembroke (*c.* 1200)
*Skenfrith, Monmouthshire
  (*c.* 1220–40)
*Tretower, Breconshire
  (*c.* 1250)

CURTAIN WITH RECTANGULAR TOWERS

*Framlingham, Suffolk (1190–1200)

CURTAINS WITH ROUNDED TOWERS AND GATEHOUSE

Bungay, Suffolk (*c.* 1294)
Corfe, Dorset
*Criccieth, Caernarvonshire
(*c.* 1220–40)
*Dover, Kent (1230–40)
*Ewloe, Flintshire (*c.* 1257)
*Goodrich, Herefordshire
(*c.* 1300)

*Pevensey, Sussex (*c.* 1250)
*Skenfrith, Monmouthshire
(*c.* 1220–40)
Skipton, Yorkshire
*White Castle, Monmouth-
shire (1220–40)
Whittington, Shropshire—
and many others

EDWARDIAN CASTLES OF WALES

Aberystwyth, Cardiganshire
(1277–*c.* 1287)
*Beaumaris, Anglesey
(1295–*c.* 1330)
*Caernarvon (1283–*c.* 1330)
*Caerphilly, Glamorgan
Chirk, Denbighshire
*Conway, Caernarvonshire
(1283–89)
*Denbigh (*c.* 1290–*c.* 1311)

*Flint (1277–86)
*Harlech, Merioneth
(1283–90)
Hawarden, Flintshire
Hope, Flintshire (1282)
*Kidwelly, Carmarthenshire
(*c.* 1275–1325)
*Rhuddlan, Flintshire
(1277–82)
Ruthin, Denbighshire
(1277–*c.* 1282)

GREAT GATEHOUSES

*Donnington, Berkshire (1385)
*Dunstanburgh, Northumberland
(*c.* 1314)
*Llanstephan, Carmarthenshire

Saltwood, Kent (1383)
Tonbridge, Kent (*c.* 1280)

GREAT TOWERS ON MOUNDS

*Clifford's Tower, York (1245)
Dudley, Worcestershire (*c.* 1310)

*Warkworth, Northumber-
land (*c.* 1300)

DEFENDED MANOR HOUSES

*Ashby de la Zouch
Leicestershire (1474)
Bolton, Yorkshire
*Kirby Muxloe, Leicestershire
(1481–4)
Leeds, Kent
Maxstoke, Warwickshire (1346)
*Nunney, Somerset (1373)
*Old Wardour, Wiltshire (1393)

*Raglan, Monmouthshire
(1430–45)
Stokesay, Shropshire (1291)
Tattershall, Lincolnshire
(1434–46)
Thornbury, Gloucestershire
(1511–21)
*Wingfield Manor, Derby-
shire (1441–55)

CASTLES FOR COASTAL DEFENCE

Bodiam, Sussex (1386)
Caister by Yarmouth, Norfolk
   (c. 1435)
Cooling, Kent (1381–4)

*Dartmouth, Devon
   (1481–94)
Herstmonceux, Sussex
   (1441)

CASTLES FOR COASTAL DEFENCE, c. 1540

*Deal, Kent
*Hurst, Hampshire
*Pendennis, Cornwall

*St Mawes, Cornwall
*Walmer, Kent

TOWN WALLS OF WHICH THERE ARE SUBSTANTIAL REMAINS

*Caernarvon
*Chepstow
 Chester
*Conway
*Denbigh
 Exeter
 Great Yarmouth

*London
 Newcastle upon Tyne
 Norwich
 Oxford
 Southampton
 Tenby
 York

The following castles are of especial interest for the many periods of
construction of which there are remains:

 Alnwick, Northumberland
 Caldicot, Monmouthshire
*Carisbrooke, Isle of Wight
*Chepstow, Monmouthshire
*Dover, Kent

*Kenilworth, Warwickshire
 Ludlow, Shropshire
 Saltwood, Kent
*Tower of London
*Warkworth, Northumberland

Plans

The following series of plans is roughly
in chronological order and is designed to
illustrate the development of fortification
from the eleventh to the sixteenth century

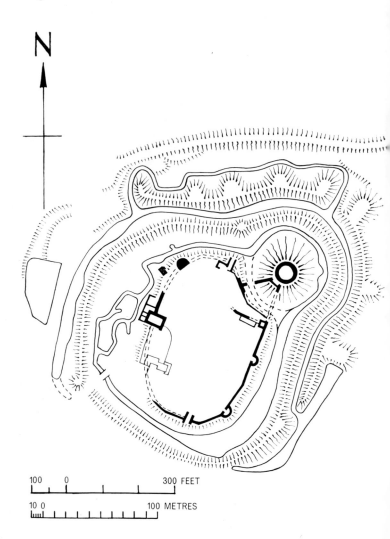

Fig. 1. Berkhamsted Castle, Hertfordshire.
Motte of 11th century with later shell keep upon it; extensive outworks, perhaps 13th-century siege-works

N

100   0   300 FEET
10 0   100 METRES

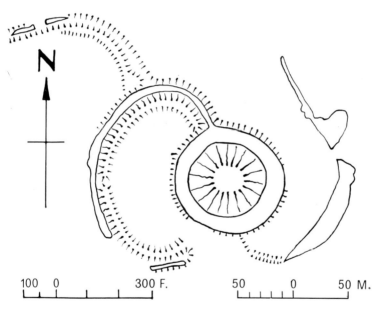

Fig. 2. Ongar Castle, Essex.
Motte of 11th or 12th century
with two or more baileys

N

100 0   300 F.

50   0   50 M.

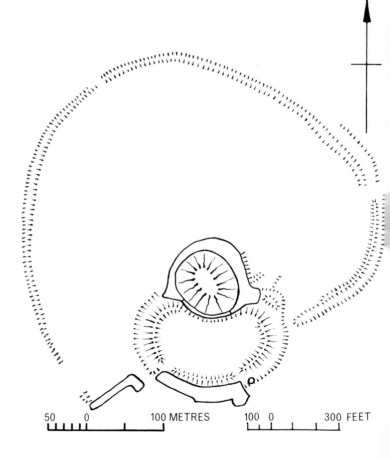

Fig. 3. Pleshey Castle, Essex.
Motte of 11th or 12th century,
with bailey and town defence

N

50   0   100 METRES   100 0   300 FEET

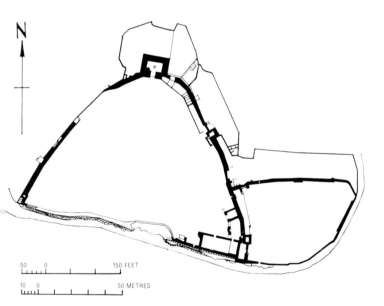

Fig. 4. Richmond Castle,
Yorkshire.
Stone curtain of 11th century with
contemporary gatehouse at
northern apex of courtyard,
which in 12th century became
a keep

N

50   0   150 FEET

10   0   50 METRES

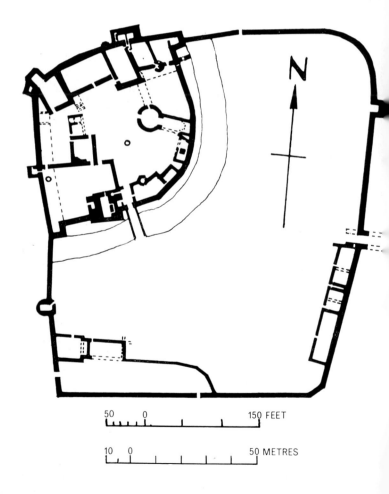

*Fig. 5. Ludlow Castle, Shropshire.
Stone curtain of inner courtyard
with small square towers, all of
11th century, with much later work*

50   0   150 FEET

10   0   50 METRES

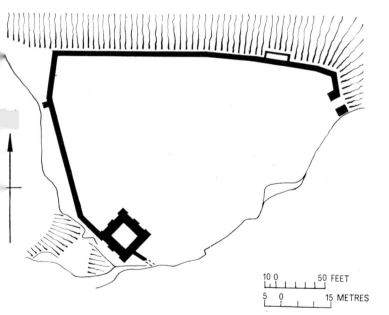

Fig. 6. Peveril Castle, Derbyshire. North curtain of 11th century; keep of 1176–7 (other buildings omitted)

10 0   50 FEET

5   0   15 METRES

*Fig. 7. Restormel Castle,
Cornwall.
Gateway of 11th century; curtain
(shell keep) of 12th century*

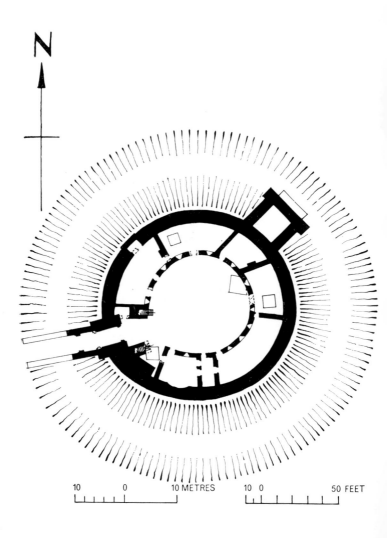

N

10 0 10 METRES   10 0   50 FEET

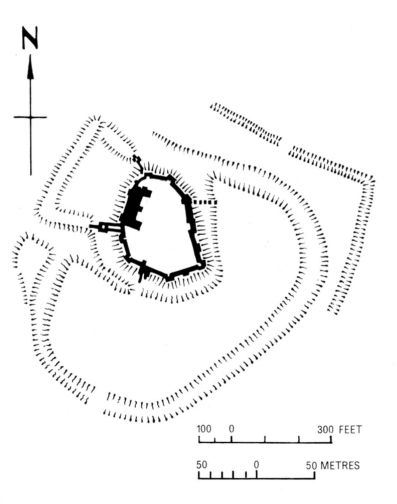

Fig. 8. Framlingham Castle, Suffolk.
High curtain with many rectangular towers, 1190–1200

N

100 0   300 FEET

50   0   50 METRES

Fig. 9. Portchester Castle, Hampshire.
Late Roman wall with towers surrounds large courtyard. In north-west corner are keep and curtain and other medieval buildings

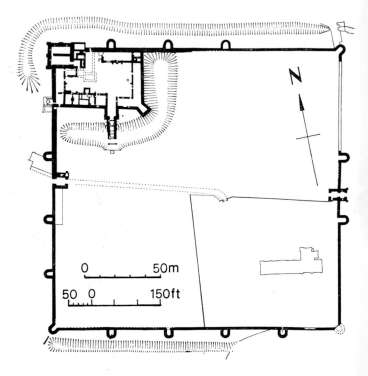

0   50m

50   0   150ft

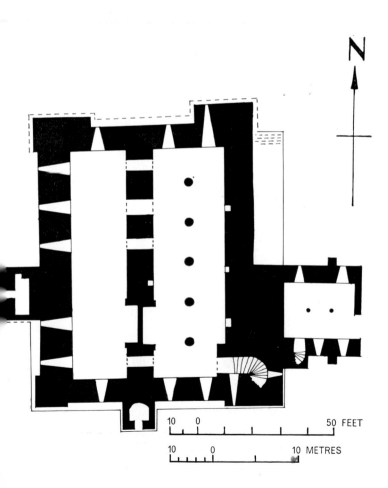

*Fig. 10. Middleham Castle,
Yorkshire.
Ground floor of keep,* c. *1170*

N

10 0   50 FEET

10   0   10 METRES

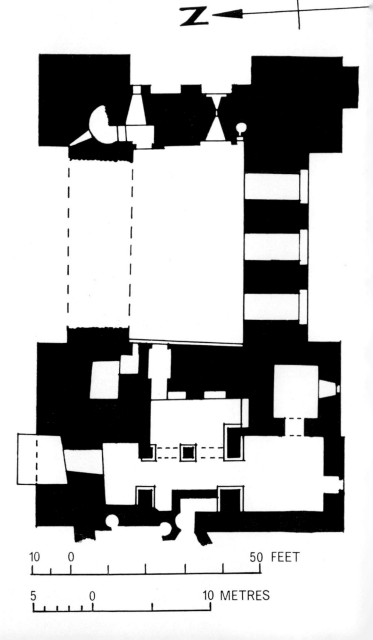

Fig. 11. Kenilworth Castle,
Warwickshire.
Ground floor of keep, 1160–80

N

| 10 | 0 | | 50 FEET |

| 5 | 0 | 10 METRES |

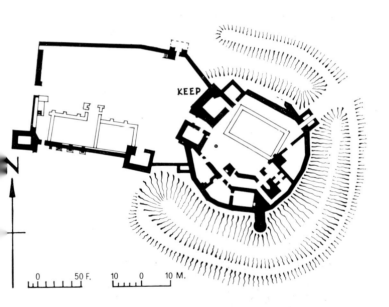

Fig. 12. Coity Castle,
Glamorgan.
Keep and polygonal curtain of
eastern ward of late 12th
century

KEEP

0   50 F.   10   0   10 M.

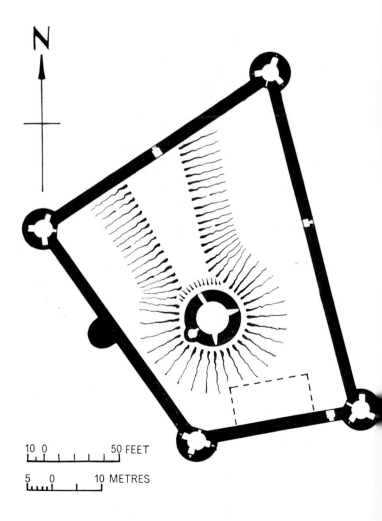

Fig. 13. Skenfrith Castle, Monmouthshire. Round keep and curtain, both of c. 1220–40

N

10 0   50 FEET

5 0   10 METRES

Fig. 14. Dolbadarn Castle,
Caernarvonshire.
Round keep of c. *1220*

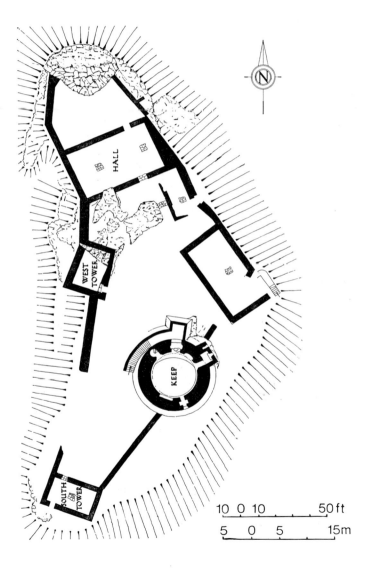

HALL

WEST TOWER

KEEP

SOUTH TOWER

N

10 0 10   50 ft

5 0 5   15m

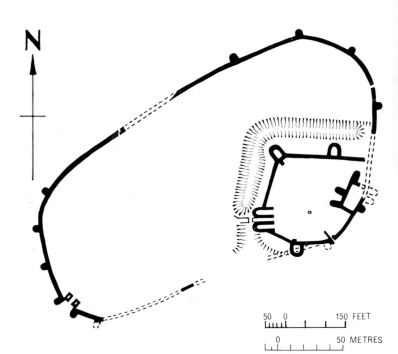

*Fig. 15. Pevensey Castle, Sussex.
Late Roman wall encloses large
outer ward. Keep in south-east
corner of 1101–30: inner
curtain c. 1250*

N

50 0   150 FEET

0   50 METRES

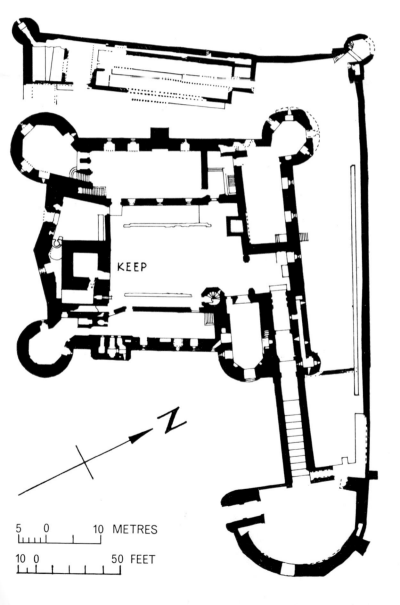

*Fig. 16. Goodrich Castle,
Herefordshire.
Keep of late 12th century;
curtain, towers and gatehouse of
c. 1300*

KEEP

N

5   0   10 METRES

10 0   50 FEET

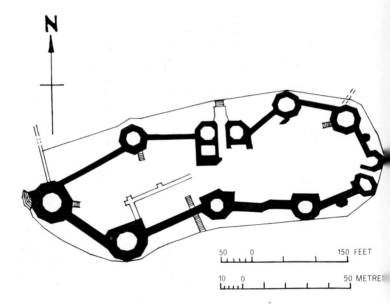

Fig. 17. Caernarvon Castle,
*1283–*c. *1330*

N

50   0   150 FEET

10   0   50 METRES

Fig. 18. Beaumaris Castle,
Anglesey, 1295–c. 1330

SEE GLOSSARY.

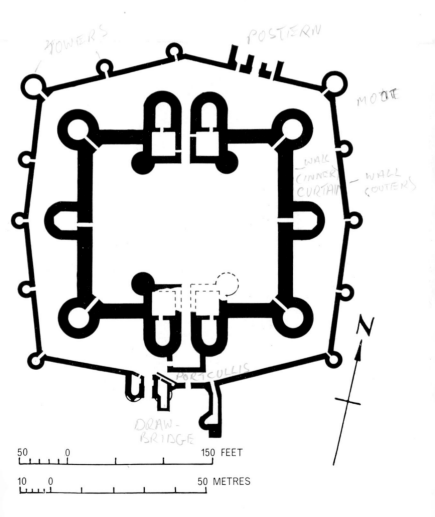

TOWERS

POSTERN

MOAT

WALK
(INNER
CURTAIN — WALL
(OUTER)

N

PORTCULLIS

DRAW-
BRIDGE

50   0   150 FEET

10 0   50 METRES

Fig. 19. Southampton Town Wall.
12th to 14th centuries

N

50   0   50 M.

0   300 F.

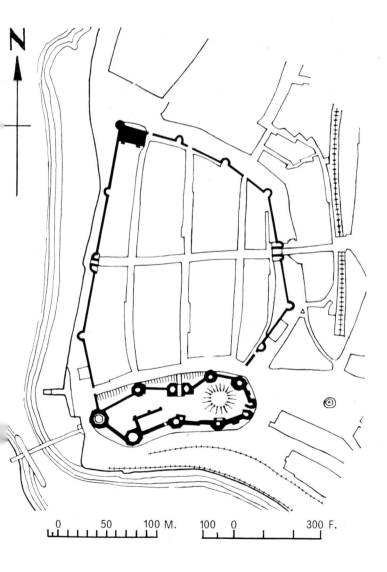

Fig. 20. Caernarvon Castle and Town Wall.
Late 13th and early 14th centuries

N

| 0 | 50 | 100 M. | 100 | 0 | 300 F. |

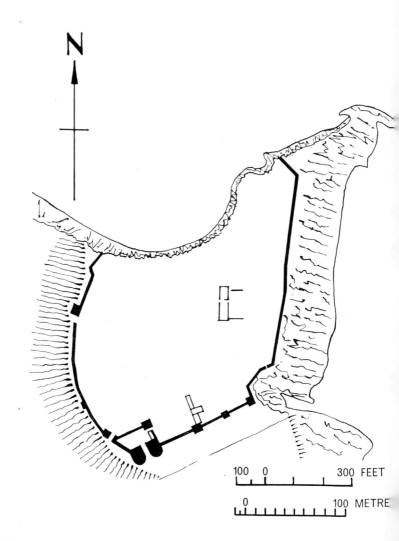

Fig. 21. Dunstanburgh Castle,
Northumberland.
Gatehouse of c. 1314

N

100   0   300 FEET

0   100 METRE

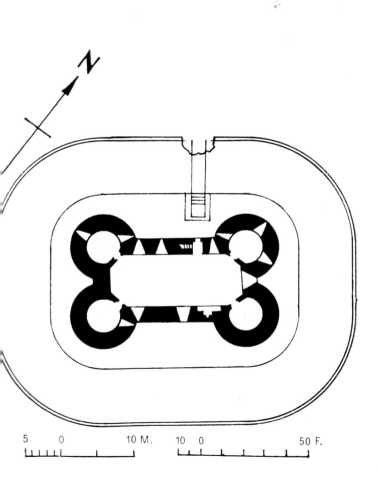

Fig. 22. Nunney Castle, Somerset, 1373

N

5   0   10 M.   10   0   50 F.

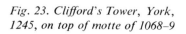

Fig. 23. Clifford's Tower, York, 1245, on top of motte of 1068–9

N

5   0   10 M.   10 0   50 F.

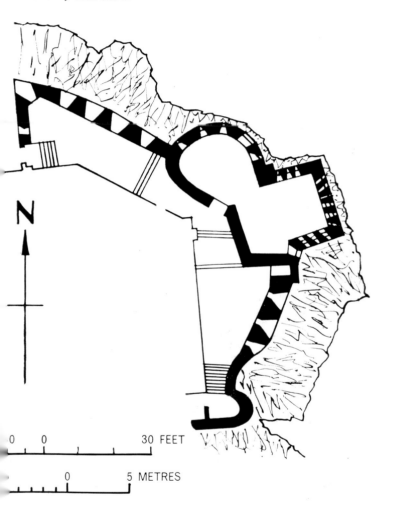

Fig. 24. Dartmouth Castle,
Devon.
Tower of 1481–94; curtain has
18th-century embrasures

N

| 0 | 0 | | 30 FEET |
| 0 | | 5 METRES | |

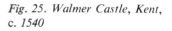

Fig. 25. Walmer Castle, Kent,
c. 1540

N

10 0   50 FEET

5   0   10 METRES

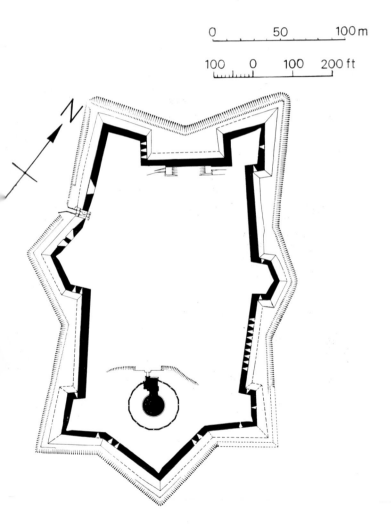

Fig. 26. Pendennis Castle, Cornwall. Inner castle c. 1540; outer ramparts late 16th century and later

0   50   100 m

100   0   100   200 ft

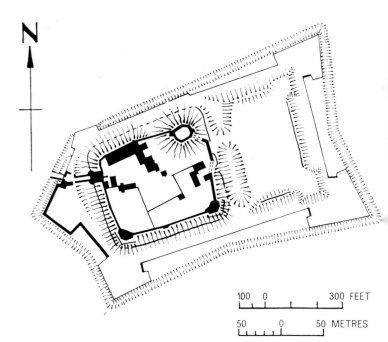

Fig. 27. Carisbrooke Castle,
Isle of Wight.
A castle of many periods:
11th-century motte, 12th-century
shell keep upon it, projecting
gatehouse of the late 15th century,
and late 16th-century ramparts
and bastions for artillery

N

100 0   300 FEET

50   0   50 METRES

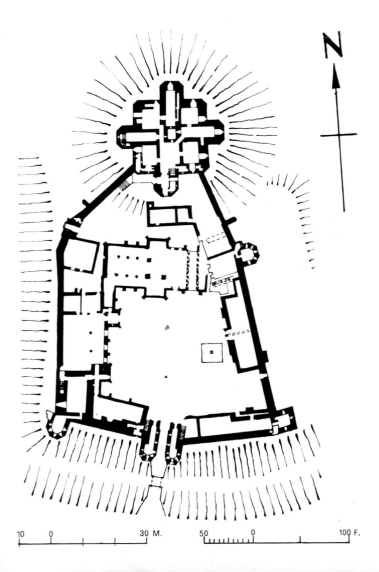

Fig. 28. Warkworth Castle, Northumberland.
A castle of many periods: an 11th- or 12th-century motte, crowned by a late 14th-century strong tower, and a church of the latter date as well as contemporary and earlier work in the curtain

N

10   0   30 M.   50   0   100 F.

Glossary

Terms used in description of castles

Bailey	Courtyard or ward.
Ballista	Machine, in the form of a very large bow, for the discharge of heavy arrows or stones.
Barbican	An outward extension of a gateway.
Belfry	A tall wooden tower, which could be moved up against the wall of castle or town in time of siege.
Berm	The flat space between the base of the curtain and the inner edge of the ditch.
Bore	A heavy pole with iron head, with which besiegers attacked the base of a wall.
Catapult	A large stone-throwing engine.
Corbel	A projection from a wall, intended to support a weight.
Crenellation	Opening in the upper part of a parapet; a sign of fortification, *e.g.* a licence to crenellate was the equivalent of a permit to fortify a residence.
Curtain	The wall enclosing a courtyard.
Donjon	Great Tower or keep. *N.B.*: the modern word dungeon is derived from donjon, but has a very different meaning.
Drawbridge	A wooden bridge, which can be raised towards a gateway by means of chains or ropes attached to its outer end.
Embrasure	A splayed opening in a wall for a window; also used as the equivalent of crenellation (see above).
Forebuilding	An additional building against a keep, in which is the stair to the doorway and sometimes a chapel.
Garderobe	Latrine.
Hall	The principal room in a medieval house.
Hoards	Also Hourds. Covered wooden galleries attached to the top of the external wall of a castle for defence of the base of the wall. They were supported on wooden brackets, the horizontal holes for which may sometimes be seen.
Keep	Great Tower or donjon; normally used of eleventh- and twelfth-century buildings, but sometimes applied loosely to those of later date.
Machicolation	An opening between corbels of a parapet or in a floor, through which a garrison could assail besiegers with missiles; or a projection containing such an opening or openings.
Mangonel	A stone-throwing engine.
Merlon	Expanses of parapet wall between embrasures; sometimes pierced with slits.
Motte	A castle mound of earth or turf (eleventh–twelfth centuries).
Pent	Also Pentise, Penthouse or lean-to.
Portcullis	An iron-shod wooden grille suspended by chains in grooves in front of a gate, and let down to ground level in times of necessity.
Postern	A back door.

Ram	Battering-ram
Sap	Undermining of a wall, above or below ground.
Screens	Wooden partition at the lower or kitchen end of a hall. Between it and the kitchen, etc., lay the screens passage.
Slit	Arrow-slit, a narrow opening in a wall for discharge of arrows and admittance of light.
Solar	A sitting-room, adjacent to the upper end of a hall.
Trebuchet	A siege engine in the form of a giant sling.
Turning-bridge	A wooden bridge pivoted on an axle and working like a see-saw, with a counterpoise weight attached to the end nearer the gateway.
Ward	Courtyard or bailey.

*The following guides to Ancient Monuments in the care
of the Department of the Environment cover England,
Wales and Scotland in five volumes, and are published
by Her Majesty's Stationery Office.*

1. NORTHERN ENGLAND   30p   (34p)
2. SOUTHERN ENGLAND   60p   (67p)
3. EAST ANGLIA AND MIDLANDS   55p   (60$\frac{1}{2}$p)
4. WALES   75p   (83$\frac{1}{2}$p)
6. SCOTLAND   Paperbound   30p   (35$\frac{1}{2}$p)
               Clothbound   50p   (58$\frac{1}{2}$p)

Other volumes on Ancient Monuments are:

ABBEYS   40p (45$\frac{1}{2}$p)
CASTLES   35p (40$\frac{1}{2}$p)
SCOTTISH ABBEYS   60p (67p)
SCOTTISH BORDER ABBEYS   15p (19p)
SCOTTISH CASTLES   27$\frac{1}{2}$p (33p)

Prices in brackets include postage

Government publications can be purchased from the Government Bookshops
in London (post orders to P.O. Box 569, SE1 9NH), Edinburgh, Cardiff,
Belfast, Manchester, Birmingham and Bristol, or through booksellers.

Printed in England for Her Majesty's Stationery Office
by William Clowes & Sons, Limited, London, Beccles and Colchester

Dd 505326 K224 3/74